W9-AXB-410

THE WRITER'S GUIDE TO

Everyday Life
in the
Middle Ages

SHERRILYN KENYON

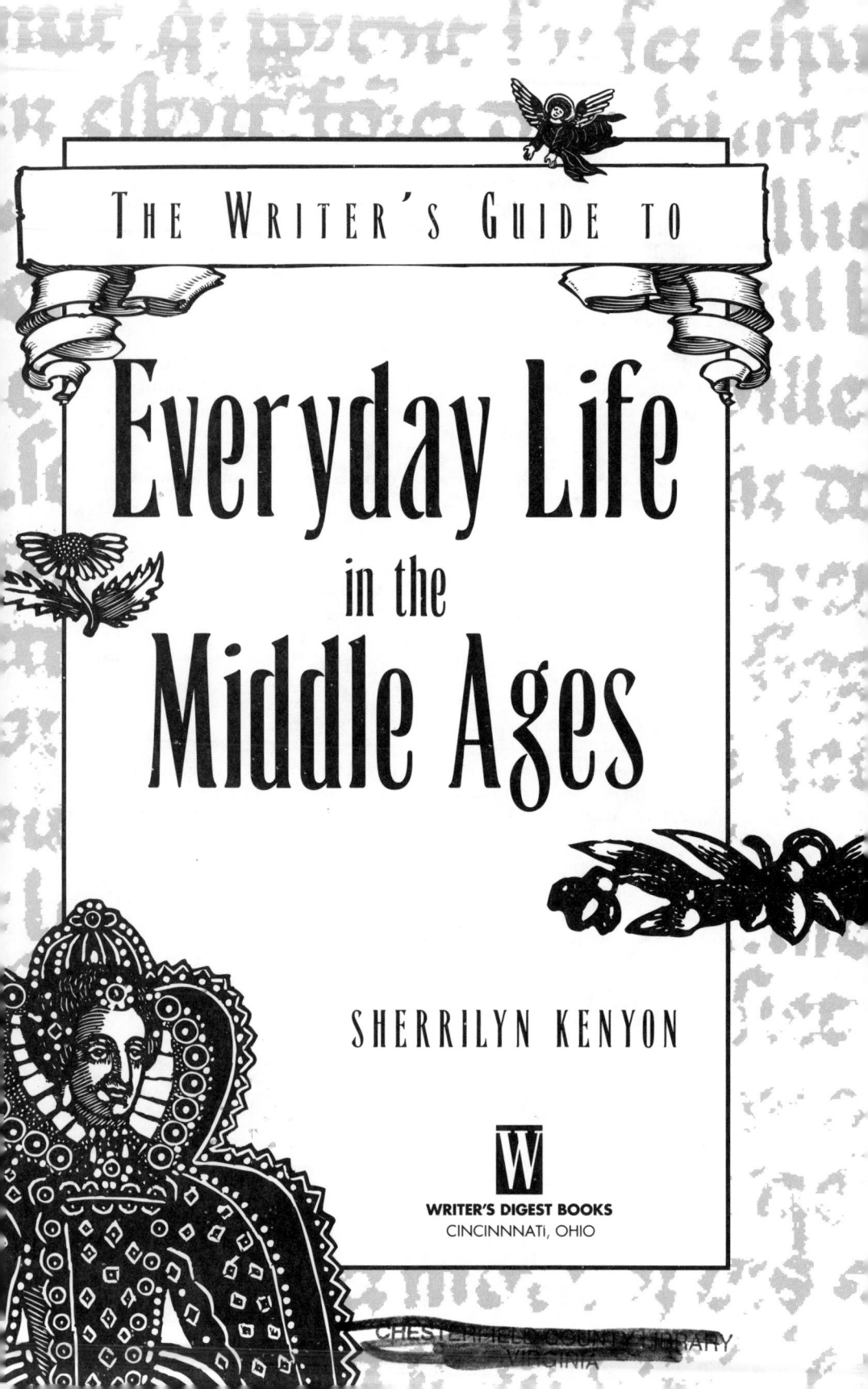

WRITER'S DIGEST BOOKS
CINCINNNATi, OHIO

This hardcover edition of **The Writer's Guide to Everyday Life in the
Middle Ages** features a "self-jacket" that eliminates the need for a
separate dust jacket. It provides sturdy protection for your book while
it saves paper, trees and energy.

Other fine Writer's Digest Books are available from your local book-
store or direct from the publisher.

99   98   97   96   5   4   3   2

Library of Congress Cataloging-in-Publication Data

Kenyon, Sherrilyn
    The writer's guide to everyday life in the Middle Ages / Sherrilyn
Kenyon—1st ed.
        p.   cm.
    Includes bibliographical references and index.
    ISBN 0-89879-663-6
    1. Historical fiction—Authorship—Handbooks, manuals, etc. 2.
Middle Ages—Historiography—Handbooks, manuals, etc. 3. Civili-
zation, Medieval—Handbooks, manuals, etc. 4. Authorship—Hand-
books, manuals, etc. I. Title. II. Title: Everyday life in the Middle
Ages.
PN3377.5.H57K46   1995
909.07—dc20   94-43915
                                                            CIP
                                                            AC

Edited by Jack Heffron
Designed by Sandy Conopeotis
Cover Design by Sandy Conopeotis

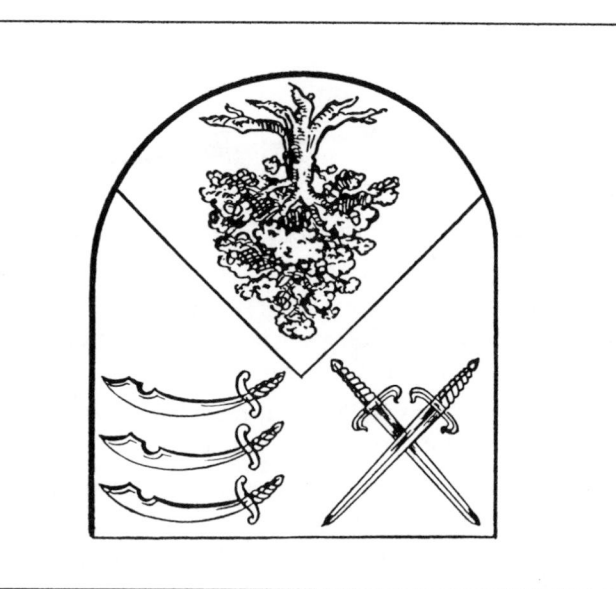

DEDICATION

In memory of Dr. James W. Alexander, who always had time for an eager student's questions. His warm encouragement and insightful comments are sorely missed.

For my mother, who placed that silly suit of armor in the den and captured a young girl's imagination.

My father, who was my first knight in shining armor.

My brother, Steve, who has always been my own special court jester.

My sister, Cathe, who read me *Robin Hood* until she was nearly mad.

And for Ken, who has been my sounding board and devil's advocate these last few years, and who has never allowed me to get away with an unfounded conclusion. Thank you.

ACKNOWLEDGMENTS

DR. VICTORIA CHANDLER, who introduced me to the Haskins Society and who has answered and directed me too many times to count.

DR. TRACY FESSENDEN, who read over sections of the manuscript and made suggestions.

DR. JUDITH KRABBE, who graciously donated her medieval bibliography and whose intelligence, encouragement and smile always inspire me. You are a true role model!

MS. HARMON at Millsaps College Library, who was so kind and prompt at getting the resources I needed.

RICKEY MALLORY, who assisted with the illustrations and without whom I would have lost my mind.

KIM HENSON JONES and the pictures she graciously donated. *Je t'aime, ma soeur.*

TANYA ANNE CROSBY, whose invaluable insight and suggestions were worth their weight in platinum.

MY HUSBAND, KEN, who never shuddered at the money I spent on research materials and books.

TO THE MEMBERS OF THE SCA and all the years of fun, experience and education they have provided. *May Goddes love blest ye alle!*

AND TO ALL THE MEDIEVAL HISTORIANS AND GRAD STUDENTS I have conversed with on various internet topics who have challenged me, expanded my conclusions, and forced me to defend my positions.

Special Acknowledgments

John Struchen and the entire staff and participants of the Georgia Renaissance Festival, who allowed pictures of their annual event in Fairburn, Georgia. Anyone interested in more information can contact them at: Georgia Renaissance Festival, P.O. Box 986, Fairburn, GA 30213

And to Pat Alderson, Terry Moss and Hank Reinhardt of Museum Replicas Ltd., who graciously donated photographs from their weaponry catalog that specializes in authentic replicas of medieval and renaissance costumes and weapons. For more information: Museum Replicas, P.O. Box 840, Conyers, GA 30207, (404)922-3700

ABOUT THE AUTHOR

Sherrilyn Kenyon has taught a number of classes and workshops in medieval history and writing. Her love of things medieval began at age five when her sister read Howard Pyle's *The Merry Adventures of Robin Hood* to her. At age sixteen, she joined the Society for Creative Anachronism to which she still belongs.

While an undergraduate at the University of Georgia, she became a member of the Charles Homer Haskins Society for medieval historians. She is also a member of the Archaeological Institute of America and an assisting editor for *The Medieval Chronicle*.

Her past works include: *Writer's Digest Character Naming Sourcebook*, and the novels, *Paradise City* and *Daemon's Angel*.

INTRODUCTION

Madame, that throgh your newfangelnesse
Many a servaunt have put out of your grace,
I take my leve of your unstedfastnesse
For wel I woot, while ye have lyves space,
Ye kan not love ful half yere in a place;
To newe thing your lust is ay so kene;
Instede of blew, ye may wel were al grene.

So wrote Geoffrey Chaucer in his poem "Against Women Unconstant." Middle English is a fascinating language. When you first hear it, it sounds remarkably foreign. Indeed, I could just as easily be quoting:

Une aventure vus dirai
Dunt li Bretun firent un lai.
Laustic ad nun, ceo m'est vis,
Si l'apelent en lur païs;
Ceo est russignol en franceis
E nihtegale en dreit engleis

Which is Marie de France's twelfth century French Lai *Laüstic*. In hearing the languages, you'll notice they have a great deal in common. After all, with the Norman invasion of 1066, the Germanic Old English was altered forever. Yet even the Medieval French has some holdovers from its Germanic roots. Note the umlauts in the excerpt from *Laüstic*.

Both languages are a bridge from their original roots to the ones we know today. This is one reason why Middle English fascinates me so. After all, it links modern English and Old English.

Littered throughout Middle English, we find Germanic pronunciations and spellings. And littered in modern English, we find a number of Old English words that survive intact with only a slight pronunciation difference: cwene (queen), cyng (king), lust, ken, wisdom, templ (temple) and lytel (little).

So why this focus on language? After all, no one will be writing a book in Old English, Middle English or Medieval French.

Simple. At first glance, the past, much like the above languages, looks complicated, almost unintelligible. Yet if you look at it in pieces as opposed to the whole, what you find are things we do know, things we do understand such as the Old English words above.

Richard Barber in *Henry Plantagenet* wrote that:

Eight centuries separate us from the age of Henry II. With each year's passing our links with the Plantagenet's times grow fewer and more slender, and the obstacles to understanding the thoughts and ways of a man living in his circumstances becomes correspondingly greater.

Where there are historians who concur, I am of the opposing school. True, eight centuries do separate us, but eight hundred years on an evolutionary scale amounts to a microsecond on a twenty-four hour clock — an amount of time so infinitesimal as to be ridiculous.

Just as we can look back on the language and recognize it, so too can we not only understand, but sympathize with Henry II and his situation. We all know what it's like to have something valuable taken from us. Those who run corporations or small businesses, or farmers who have had others take what they've built, know exactly what it's like to lose important property. Though the above is not a kingdom, we can still understand Henry's driving need to retake his promised lands from Stephen.

And the events of his later life are just as understandable. Most parents can relate to having children rebel against them. This happens every day, especially in cases of powerful or rich families where the children are eager for their inheritance.

Or what about Eleanor siding with her children against Henry? Again, this is not unusual. So wherein lies this mysterious element that prevents us from understanding Henry's circumstances and thoughts?

Just like us, he was a human being; he lived, he fought, he struggled, he died.

It is what I term the fallacy of the human ego that makes us look to the past and proudly proclaim our superiority. Have we truly changed so much? Is there a shred of truth to the thought that no other past generation traveled the ground we travel now?

No. In fact, this argument is the same one voiced by teenagers who refuse to believe their parents ever had a youth, ever faced peer pressure or being stood up.

By reading the literature and letters of the medieval period, a researcher is quickly struck by parallels. Let's examine for a moment two twelfth century letters translated by Catherine Moriarity:

To their dear and respected parents M. Marte, knight

and M. his wife, M. and S., their sons, send greetings and filian obedience.

This is to inform you that, by divine mercy, we are living in good health in the city of Orleans and are devoting ourselves wholly to study, mindful of the words of Cato, 'To know anything is praiseworthy,' etc. We occupy a good and comely dwelling, next door but one to the schools and market place, so that we can go to school every day without wetting our feet. We have also good companions in the house with us, well advanced with their studies and of excellent habits — an advantage which we well appreciate, for as the Psalmist says, 'With an upright man, thou wilt show thyself upright' etc. Wherefore lest production cease from lack of material, we beg your paternity to send us by the bearer, B., money for buying parchment, ink, desk, and the other things which we need, in sufficient amount that we may suffer no want on your account (God Forbid!) but finish our studies and return home with honour. The bearer will also take charge of the shoes and stockings which you have to send us, and any news as well.

I know my father relates to that letter. Instead of quoting Psalms, I used terms like Pseudo-Isodorian Decretels and quoted Plato to show him his money wasn't being wasted. Indeed, I think any student or parent can relate to the old, "But Mom, Dad, everyone else has a new notebook! How can I keep up with them if all I have is my ratty one from last year?"

And like most parents who lose patience with their children who seem to idle a bit, here's another letter. This one is from Besancon to his son:

It is written, 'He also that is slothful in his work is brother to him that is a great waster.' I have recently discovered that you loved dissolutely and slothfully, preferring license to restraint and play to work and strumming the guitar while the others are at their studies, whence it happens that you have read but one volume of law while your more industrious companions have read several. Wherefore I have decided to exhort you herewith to repent utterly of your dissolute and careless ways that you

3

may no longer be called a waster and that your shame
may be turned to good repute.

Again, I think most people can relate to this message!

So how is it that myths and misconceptions get started? Why do people often say, "Oh, how medieval!" as if that is the most backwards thing anything can be?

Well, there is a lot of history that does separate us from the Middle Ages, and sometimes it's easy to throw all history into one category and to draw generalizations where generalizations should not be drawn. If we in our modern twentieth century had to fight for women's rights, then it is only natural that we are the first to have them.

Actually, women of the past had far more authority than most women today. For example, can an average woman today hold a legal court and expect her sentence to be carried out? Can an average woman lead an army? Can an average woman hire or fire her children's teachers? Of course not. Yet these are typical duties expected of noblewomen, and in certain cases, middle-class women, in the medieval period.

But what of the laws and church writings that said women had to subjugate themselves to their husbands? Let's take a moment to look at our own laws. How many of us pay attention to jay-walking ordinances? Speeding laws? And even with the stiff penalties against driving while intoxicated, how many people every day drive under the influence of some drug? Medieval people were no different. Some obeyed the laws, some didn't, and some didn't even know what the laws were. An example of this comes from Patricia Orr's research on the years 1194 to 1232. She came across a reference that says no woman could bring a case to a royal court unless it involved personal injury to herself or the death of her husband. Yet only three cases were ever dismissed on these grounds, while literally hundreds of others were heard regarding everything from theft to murder.

Where it is true that we will never know the exact truth of how women were treated, I think we can draw a close parallel with our own society. Some women were loved and treasured and some were horribly abused. And just as some were abused, others were abusers. There are a number of cases of women who neglected and abused their husbands and children.

And though there were laws granting the husband the right to punish his wife, he was never supposed to hit her in anger or while drinking. As disturbing as this law may be to some, I hasten to remind everyone that this view can still be found in modern society. In fact, I heard a female caller not long ago on a local talk show say that she thought a husband had a right to punish his wife if the wife deserved it, and this caller was in her twenties.

So why are there so many discrepancies out there? Why do we pick up J.W. Thompson's *Economic and Social History of the Middle Ages* and read that no woman was ever a peddler in the Middle Ages? Then we pick up Maryanne Kowaleski and Judith M. Bennett's article, "Crafts, Gilds, and Women in the Middle Ages: Fifty Years After Marian K. Dale," which says there were a number of women who peddled for a living?

One reason can be found in the dates. Thompson's book is from 1952, whereas Kowaleski and Bennett's article was written in 1989. In thirty years, a lot of important research has been done. New documents and archaeological finds have completely rewritten certain historical beliefs.

In 1961 when Sidney Painter died, his lifelong dream had been to research and write on medieval marriage, a much neglected subject in those days. A few years after that, Georges Duby took the torch and produced two books and a number of articles on the subject. Today we have a larger number of books, papers and articles to draw from.

For this reason, I strongly advise researchers to focus on newer books. True, there is a great deal of value to be found in older works such as those by G.C. Coulton, F.W. Maitland, Henri Pirenne and others. But older books also contain outdated research and thoughts such as Henri Pirenne's statement that the Germanic hordes did not destroy the Roman Empire that "they barbarized it, but they did not consciously germanize it." Though there is some truth to this, the bulk of the sentiment has long since been cast aside. Most modern historians are quick to point out that the hordes had no interest in preserving Roman tradition. Instead they wanted to partake of the riches and advantages of being citizens, but they wanted their own language and laws.

So where does this leave a modern writer, someone who doesn't have time to read every book written on the Middle Ages? Actually, the discrepancies and opposing arguments offer a writer great fodder for a story. Take for a moment Karen Armstrong's theory that the Children's Crusade wasn't a group of children who left for the Holy Land where they either died or were sold into slavery, but was in fact a group of peasants who protested in the countryside for one summer. Depending on which theory a writer uses, there are multiple story line possibilities.

There is nothing easy about the Middle Ages. It was as complex a time as the years we now live in. Society constantly shifted, as did laws, fashions and beliefs. Indeed, many things we now take for granted were formed in the medieval period: purgatory (thirteenth century), marriage as a sacrament (twelfth century), surnames (developed all throughout the period), universities (tenth century), hospitals and more. Even ninety percent of all the classical writings that survive today come down to us only through medieval manuscript copies.

For this reason, I urge all writers to be careful of what old beliefs about the Middle Ages they hold. Just like old wives' tales, these commonly held beliefs can be misleading or incorrect. Only careful research will prevent embarrassing mistakes.

This book is designed as a mere starting point or as a reference to look up much needed information as quickly as possible. Each section offers a brief overview of the subject and should be treated only as such.

Though I have tried to be as thorough as possible and to present facts objectively, I realize that at times I have inserted my own views drawn from my own research. And as with all historical works, time and space prevented me from exploring all angles and arguments.

I would also like to note that though I've had professors and colleagues review my work and have followed some of their guidance, ultimately I had to make the decision on what to include and on what view I hold on certain issues. This book is a reflection of my research, not theirs.

I wish all writers much success with their historical endeavors, and I hope this book provides the reading lists and necessary information to make those books as accurate as possible.

et les chualco...
...fore our. biene fanne.
a uefta et apareihe fe li...
moi fire chr. er il li fift er...
rout au hege pilleus. x le...
...er bene le... dont il e...
...u uou fere...
...deu...
...no regar... les le...
...ue le noma...
...ent. Sur. chr. afee...
...rit... la fift ror...
...ap...ome...
er. ana fer et...
lua mo...

PART ONE

Everyday Life

In·ardua·tendit

CHAPTER ONE

FOOD

ood in a castle was served in the great hall, a large room usually on an upper floor. The lord's table was set up along one wall on a small dias, the rest of the tables were positioned in a perpendicular fashion to the lord's dias. Lower tables were called trestle tables, and when the meals were not being eaten, these tables were taken down and stacked in designated areas. The lord, his guests and family who all sat at the lord's table were the only ones to have chairs; everyone else sat on a bench.

Breakfast was a small snack usually served after morning mass. It consisted of a hunk of bread and ale or cider for the retainers and servants. The lord, his family and guests might be served white bread with a cold slice of meat, cheese and wine.

Dinner, served between 10:00 A.M. and noon, was the main meal of the day. A trumpeter or crier would announce the meal at a castle. When a guest entered, the ladies would curtsey and take their seats. The lord might give the guest a light, quick kiss before showing the guest to his seat at the lord's table.

Attendants or pages would bring a washbowl forward and pour water for the guest and lord out of an aquanmanile (an elaborate pitcher). The rest of the diners would wash their hands in a lavabo-type dispenser in the great hall and dry their hands on a long towel. They would then take their seats at the lower trestle tables on benches that often served as their beds at night.

The diners were served in order: first the visiting clergy, the visiting nobles, the lord and his family, then the retainers.

Table settings included a silver salt cellar, a nef and cups. The cups were made of silver, pewter, wood or horn, though the wealthy could have cups made of coconut shells, ostrich eggs, agate or gourds. Spoons were provided, but guests were expected to bring their own knives to table (forks did not appear until the late fourteenth century and weren't commonly used until the Renaissance).

Either wooden bowls were set out with a thick slice, or chunk, of bread lining the bottom, or round bread would be scooped out to form a bowl. The lord and his guests usually had a silver platter and the rest of the diners were served from wooden platters (one platter was shared by two people). From these platters, the food was placed upon a trencher to be eaten. Platters were used solely for serving.

A large trencher made of bread was set on the table (one for every two people). One person sliced the trencher and kept half, and the other person used the second half as a plate. Plates are not found in England until the very end of the fourteenth century.

Dinner began with a blessing from the chaplain followed by a procession led from the unoccupied side of the lord's table by the steward who oversaw the staff. Next came the pantler who distributed bread and butter, the butler and his assistants who poured the wine, beer or ale, and the kitchen assistants who brought in the rest of the first course. A course was cleared completely from the tables before the next was brought in.

Food was either carried up from a lower level of the castle, or brought in from a separate building. As a result, the food was seldom, if ever, more than lukewarm.

Everyday dinners had two or three courses each, and the last course usually consisted of fruits, cheeses, nuts, wafers and spiced wine. A feast could consist of a number of courses and stagger the average person's imagination with the complexity and variety of dishes.

Pages, or cup bearers, made certain no one's cup went empty. When meat was brought into the great hall on a spit, a young gentleman carver would slice it. But since most meat was boiled, a lord or guest would indicate which meats he wanted and a servant or page would place it on his platter. From there, meat was cut and distributed between dining partners so that a lower ranking lord would serve a higher ranking lord, a man would serve a woman, and a young person would serve an elder.

Food was eaten with the fingers, except for broth, which was sipped, and some stews, which were eaten with spoons.

Before the meat was served, the bread would be broken, or the trencher sliced in half, with each person receiving an equal share.

At the end of the meal, the diners would again wash their hands and return to their duties. The trenchers and bowl liners were gathered by servants and given to the almoner who saw that they were distributed to the poor and needy.

Merchants ate in a similar fashion, but their meals were not as large, or their retainers as many. A tablecloth was draped over each table with one side longer to be used by everyone as a napkin. During a festive occasion with many courses, the tablecloth was changed between each course. Each diner had a knife, spoon and a trencher of day-old bread, which wouldn't absorb all the juices of their food as quickly as fresh-baked bread. Blessings were said by the youngest family member or by a visiting clergyman.

A bowl-shaped trencher.

A peasant's meal was much more humble. An average meal generally consisted of porridge, turnips, dark bread (only the nobility had white bread), and beer or ale. A salad might be added that would consist of parsley, borage, mint, rosemary, thyme, purslayne, garlic or fennel, and a vinegar or verjuice dressing. During hog slaughtering season, peasants would eat pork and bacon, but usually fish was the primary source of meat.

Villagers would eat bread—either rye, barley or wheat—that was occasionally mixed with peas or beans. They also enjoyed oatmeal cakes, porridge, fish, cheese curds, watery ale, mead, cider and metheglin.

Supper at the castle was a light meal served at sunset and usually consisted of one main dish, several small side dishes and cheese. After supper, castle occupants might be entertained by a traveling minstrel, acrobat, contortionist, jongleur or storyteller who performed for their food and were usually given coin as well. If no professional entertainers were present, games might be played, or the lady of the hall or a knight might provide entertainment with a song, instrument or a story.

For the lord or his family who might be absent during a meal, or for someone who came unexpectedly and might need food, bread, cold meat, meat pies, cheese and drink were kept in a livery cupboard located in or near the great hall. Some nobles even had a small livery cupboard in their personal chambers, but this was frowned on by the church as a form of gluttony.

The clergy ate only one meal a day. However, during the summer a light supper was permitted in addition to the midday meal. Each order had its own regulations about what and how much food should be eaten. The Carthusians in Germany, for example, ate vegetable platters. French Cistercian monks ate barley bread, and vetch or millet with boiled roots or nettle leaves. The Benedictines forbade meat except for the sick. On fasting days, oysters, fish and poultry were eaten.

Meals in a monastery were supposed to be eaten in silence even though many clergymen would sign to one another while eating. A lector would stand and read inspirational works during the meal.

✤ ✤ ✤

TYPES OF FOOD

Throughout the period, a variety of foods was eaten by all classes. Some of the foods (due to preservation techniques of salting and applying heavy spices to disguise rotting) would be quite unappealing to the twentieth century palate. Nobility tended to eat mostly meats and pastries. Merchants also consumed a lot of meat, but would also eat vegetables. The poor ate a diet predominately of vegetables and dark breads.

The most common vegetables (which were dubbed commoners' food) were onions, peas, beans, cabbage, parsley, shallots and potherbs. Cucumbers and leeks were avoided since most considered

A flat, sliced trencher that is shared by two people.

them unhealthy. Tomatoes, potatoes and Indian corn did not exist in Europe until the sixteenth century.

Common meats included the following:

Birds: starlings, vultures, gulls, herons, storks, cormorants, swans, cranes, peacocks, capons and chickens.

Seafood: dogfish, porpoises, seals, whale, haddock, cod, salmon, sardines, lamprey, dolphins, tunnies and eels.

Other meats: venison, mutton and pork. Horse meat was forbidden by the church.

Fruits in the Middle Ages were smaller and usually grown in the wild. Raw fruits were thought unwholesome and were seldom served. Fruits mainly consisted of apples, plums, pears, peaches and nuts. Citrus fruits, such as oranges and lemons, were not found in England until the Crusades, and even then they were rare treats. The first recorded large shipment of oranges didn't occur until the late fourteenth century.

Desserts consisted of cheeses, cakes, wafers, spiced wines, cookies, waffles and jellies.

Nobility drank wine, which was sometimes spiced to cover the taste of souring and often diluted or mixed with honey or cinnamon. Mulled wine was the only drink served hot. Lower classes drank mead, ale and beer. The clergy scented their mead with herbs and honey and sometimes added water.

All medieval dishes relied heavily on spices for a number of reasons, the largest being that spices covered the taste of spoiling meat. Garlic was used so heavily by the French that the crusaders offended the people of Constantinople with their breath!

Sugar, one of the most valuable spices, was expensive to import, but from the twelfth century onward, it was a common ingredient in England. Sugars from Alexandria were especially coveted because they were flavored with rose and violets. The most common spices were pepper, mustard, garlic, cloves, vinegar, verjuice, cinnamon, almonds and saffron. Wine and ale were often used to cook fish.

MANNERS

Since the platters and trenchers were shared among the nobility and merchant class, stringent rules of etiquette applied to table manners. People were expected to wash their hands before eating. If dining with the king, a person must bow to the nef before passing it.

People were to always wipe their mouths before taking a drink from the goblet (cups were also shared between two people). Diners ate slowly, taking small bites. They were never to speak with their mouths full, nor were they to take a drink with food still in their mouths. Knives were used for cutting and were not supposed to be placed in the mouth. Spoons were set on the table, not left in the bowl.

Diners were not to gnaw on bones with their teeth, poke their fingers in eggs, spit across the table, wipe their mouths on their sleeves, or bite into the trencher, since this was given to the poor to eat.

Like today, elbows were not supposed to be put on the table, soup was not to be slurped, and there was no belching, leaning over the food, or picking any orifice. No one was supposed to wipe their teeth or knife on the tablecloth, or butter bread with their thumbs.

Food was not to be plunked down in the salt cellar, nor was food to be blown upon to cool it (although, just as people presently do, this often went unheeded). Scraps were not to be fed to the dogs while the diners ate, and many etiquette books spoke against tossing scraps to the dogs even after the meal.

Assorted Food Facts

Food imports and exports played a vital part in trade. England exported fish, cheese and ale and imported raisins, figs, dates, olive oil, wine, almonds, rice and pomegranates. Spain was known for exporting sugar, preserved fruits and syrups. France was known for exporting wine, and Italy for pies.

Food was usually plentiful in the spring and summer, provided there were no droughts, crop failures or pillaging. In winter, cow's milk was scarce and seldom used to cook with.

To ensure survival, meats were salted and stored using one of two methods: dry salting (burying meat in salt) or brine curing (soaking meat in a salt solution). Until the fourteenth century, several types of fish were not gutted before they were preserved.

Due to the heavy amount of meats and pastries consumed by the upper classes, many health problems existed, such as skin irritations, scurvy, tooth decay, heart disease, and numerous infections from bad meat.

For main dishes, cooks paid special attention to the appearance of the food. Swans were cooked fully feathered; heads and other parts of animals were either left on or sewed on after cooking. Many subtleties (sculptures of jelly, sugar and paste) were made.

Common Dishes of Scotland and England

A few common Scottish dishes include:

- Antholl Brose: Made from ale, oatmeal and honey.
- Barley Bannocks: A type of bread made from barley, flour, salt and buttermilk.
- Carrageen Jelly: Made from seaweed and milk.
- Colcannon: A stew made from cabbage, turnips and carrots.
- Crowdie: In the Highlands, it's a type of cheese; in the Lowlands, it's milk and oatmeal.
- Forfar Bridies: A mincemeat pastry.
- Gundy: A type of candy made with sugar, butter and black treacle. Best when seasoned with cinnamon.
- Haggis: A sheep's bladder stuffed with onions, oatmeal, liver, heart and beef.
- Hotch-Potch: A type of stew made with beef or mutton.

Beverages include:

- Pirr

- Blaand
- Heather Ale
- Drammach.

In England some common dishes include:

- Stuffed Pigling—pigling stuffed with nuts, cheese, eggs, spices, bread.
- Entrayale—a dish made of sheep's stomach. The stomach is stuffed with eggs, vegetables, bread, cheese and pork.
- Lampreys in Galytyne—a type of spiced lamprey dish.
- Blackmanger—a chicken dish made with rice, almonds and sugar.
- Mortrews—a meat dish made with eggs and bread crumbs.
- Viaund Royal
- Capon de Haut de Grace
- Venison en Frumenty—venison and whole wheat boiled in milk and heavily spiced.
- Frumenty Pudding—a wheat, milk pudding.
- Leche Lumbarde
- Blaundesorye

Beverages include:

- Cowslip wine
- Dandelion wine
- Elderberry wine
- Apple beer

RECIPES

Water for washing hands: Boil sage, rosemary, bay leaves or chamomile in water. Strain, then cool and pour in a bowl.

Mead: Dissolve four pounds of honey in a gallon of water with half an ounce of ginger. Boil for approximately forty-five minutes, then pour into a barrel or wooden container. Before it cools completely, add yeast and wait for it to ferment. After fermentation, seal and store for six months.

Lampreys in Galytyne: Skin and gut a lamprey, making sure to keep the blood in another container for later use. Roast the lamprey on a spit, and save the grease. Mix ground raisins with rose petals and combine with bread crusts and vinegar, or verjuice. Add powder ginger and the blood and grease to the raisin mixture, then boil together and salt to taste.

Cheese Crowdie: Heat soured milk until it separates. Do not boil. Strain the whey. Season the solid cheese block with salt, pepper and a dab of garlic. Let stand for a day or two.

Haggis: Soak a sheep's bladder in salted water for at least twelve hours. Turn the roughened side out, then wash the small bag. Hang the windpipe over the edge of the pot. Cover with water and boil for an hour or two. Afterwards, cut off the pipe and gristle. Finely chop the heart and half of the liver. Add two chopped onions, garlic and oatmeal, and moisten with broth. Put the mixture inside the large bag and sew closed. Boil for approximately three hours, cutting a small hole when the bag begins to swell.

Eels: Skin and gut eels, then cut into chunks and place them in a pan of salted water. Add chopped parsley, garlic and pepper. Boil until the eel chunks begin to split.

Blackmanger: Cut chicken into chunks, and blend with rice that has been boiled in almond milk and salt and seasoned with sugar. Cook until mixture is very thick and garnish with anise and fried almonds.

FOR FURTHER READING

T. Austin, *Two Fifteenth Century Cookery Books*.

T. Bayard, *A Medieval Home Companion*.

M. Black, *The Medieval Cookbook*.

F.J. Furnivall, *The Babees' Book: Medieval Manners from the Young*.

J. and F. Gies, *Life in a Medieval City*.

J. and F. Gies, *Life in a Medieval Village*.

P.W. Hammond, *Food and Feast in Medieval England*.

D. Hartley, *Food in England*.

U.T. Holmes, Jr., *Daily Living in the Twelfth Century*.

CHAPTER TWO

CLOTHING

n the early Middle Ages, very little separated the dress of the nobility from that of the peasantry. The styles of clothing and the types of fabric they wore were very much alike. This similarity in dress, however, should not suggest an egalitarian society in which the nobility was uninterested in distinguishing themselves from the common folk. The similarity was due mostly to limited trade caused by poor travel conditions. Remember that the roads at this time were terrible, so merchants and peddlers could not go far with their carts and wagons. And even those roads that were passable were riddled with thieves who often killed travelers to steal their belongings.

Throughout this period, most nobles, in order to set themselves apart, relied on jewels, which were easier to obtain, especially in the North, where mining was prevalent. In the mid to late eleventh century this situation began to change. The roads gradually improved, making it easier for peddlers to move their wares from place to place. Also, the growing strength of the kings and nobles to control their domains lessened the risk of robbery and violence along the roads. This new mobility led to an increase in trade, bringing a greater variety of fabrics and colors and fashions to those who could afford them. These luxuries, of course, were too expensive for the peasants, but the wealthy seized the opportunity and their fashions began to change.

From this time forward, dress denoted stature and wealth, much as it does today. During the late Middle Ages, sumptuary laws were instituted to ensure that certain fabrics and styles were reserved for those who had a right to wear them. Fashion police would actually patrol the streets checking men and women to make sure they were wearing the appropriate clothing.

As you'll see in this chapter, fashions changed throughout the Middle Ages. To provide you with an overview of these changes, I've divided the period into units of roughly fifty to seventy years. You should not, however, conclude that fashions changed more slowly in the Middle Ages than they do today. We simply lack the space in this book to note every change as it occurred.

WOMEN

By studying manuscripts, we can infer that women's fashions did indeed change quickly. Some trends lasted for decades while others came and went in a couple of years. The women's kirtle, for example, changed from being a large, voluminous mass to a laced, form-clinging dress, the neck and sleeves of which were routinely changed. Sleeves often were detachable so that the woman could keep the main, most expensive part of the dress while still remaining fashionable. In fact, in the later Middle Ages, many women's trousseaus consisted of bolts of fabric with only a few gowns because the fashions changed so quickly that any gowns they brought to the marriage would soon be dated.

1066 to 1087

Undergarment: An under-tunic or smock was the only undergarment worn. It was an under-dress only visible when the kirtle's sleeves or hem fell short.

Hose: Gartered at the knee.

Shoes: Leather and rose to just above the ankle.

Dress: Called a kirtle.

Girdles: Long and worn around the hips.

Cloaks: Semi-circular, they were worn long and fastened by cord or brooch.

Hair: Worn long and sometimes plaited, it was covered by a long, finely woven veil that was wound about the neck. At times, a circlet was used to keep it in place.

Fabrics: Nobles wore linen and wool; peasants wore russet.

Colors: Red, green, light blue, gray, yellow, red-brown, brown, black.

1087 to 1154

Undergarment: The sleeves were full and the entire smock was "broom sticked" (twisted while wet and dried so as to achieve a crinkled effect).

Hose: Same as before.

Shoes: Same as before.

Dress: Called a kirtle or gown.

Girdles: Same as before, except at state functions a longer girdle was used. Women wrapped this around their upper waist, then doubled it in back and tied on low on their hips (1125 to 1175).

Cloaks: From the East, a *pelisse* came into fashion. It was a short, coat-like garment that fastened at the waist and hung just below the knee.

Hair: Girls wore their hair loose. After 1120, hair was wrapped in ribbon or cloth and was allowed to hang to the knee or lower. If a woman couldn't grow her hair to the fashionable length, false hair was used. Between 1120 and 1150, the veil was worn loose, down the back and secured to the head with a circlet made of gold, silver or silk.

Fabrics: The weave became finer. Nobles wore silk, linen and wool.

Colors: Red, green, light blue, blue, gray, yellow, red-brown, brown and black.

1154 to 1199

Undergarment: The smock sleeves became tight again and a little longer. If the kirtle was cut short, then the bottom of the smock would be shown.

Hose: Still gartered at the knee.

Shoes: Still cut low and made of leather.

Dress: Called a kirtle or gown.

Girdles: Not as popular during this period.

A basic kirtle. Sleeves varied according to fashion.

Cloaks: Woven with heavier material, they remain the same as before.

Hair: The plaits began to fade from fashion, though they are still found at the turn of the century. Hair was wound about the head. During the reign of Richard, the short veils became popular and were held in place by gold or silken bands. Around 1170, the barbette was introduced (page 27), and ca. 1190 the wimple came into fashion. The wimple was wound about the neck, tucked into the kirtle and was pinned to the hair.

Fabrics: Scarlet was introduced, silks, linen, heavily embroidered cloth, wool. The lower classes wore coarser wool and russet.

Colors: Scarlet, watchet, green, yellow, tawny, red, red-brown, black and gray.

1199 to 1272

Undergarment: Didn't change much, but it was no longer revealed by the nobility.

Hose: Same as before.

Shoes: Same as before.

Dress: Called a kirtle or gown.

Girdles: Leather or silk, though still not worn much at home. Long purses often dangled from them.

Cloaks: Lined with fur and embroidered.

Hair: Hair began being coiled on either side of the head. In 1216, short veils and hats returned and often concealed the hair. Around 1220, the fillet of linen was often worn with the barbette. During trips, women also wore small round hats.

Fabrics: Same as before.

Colors: Purple, scarlet, watchet, red, tawny, yellow, brown, red-brown, green, murrey and gray.

Lower classes: Aprons began to be worn and also a sleeveless super-tunic (1216 to 1272).

1272 to 1307

Undergarment: Same as before.

Hose: Same as before.

Shoes: Had pointed toes.

Dress: Called a kirtle.

Girdles: Seldom worn.

Cloaks: Made full and long, they were still made from heavier materials and lined with fur or a lighter fabric. Buttons began to replace other fasteners.

Hair: Caul and frets began to be worn. They were the thick silk or gold nets that most people associate with the period. Some women still continued to wear their hair coiled around each ear. The wimple persisted along with the shorter veil. Widows wore a pleated wimple that covered their chins. The wimple could also be worn without a veil or hat. The other types of headdresses were also still worn. Young girls and women also wore their hair loose with a silk or gold band.

Fabrics: Velvet (appeared around 1303) was reserved for royalty. Fustian, a silky material that was similar to velvet, appeared around the same time and was used for the lesser nobility. Scarlet, wool and linen were also worn. Serge also appeared at the turn of the century, but was used for outer garments. Russet, canvas and linen were used by the rest.

Colors: Purple, scarlet, murrey, watchet, green, gray, reddish brown, red, light blue, tawny, brown and slate.

1307 to 1327

Undergarment: The smock was now called the kirtle and became a visible, vital part to dressing. Sleeves were still form fitting.

Hose: Same as before.

Shoes: Same as before.

Dress: Called a surcoat.

Cloaks: Same as before, but during the period, coats of arms began to be embroidered on them.

Hair: Veils became more popular. They were either worn with a thin gold or silk band, or were draped over a wider band. The barbette fades during this period and vanishes from fashion.

Fabrics: Taffeta (very expensive), velvet, kersey, scarlet, fustian, linen, wool, russet and canvas.

Colors: Silver and gold appeared but were reserved for royalty. Purple, scarlet, murrey, watchet, green, gray, reddish brown, red, flame, white, light blue, tawny, brown and slate.

1327 to 1377

Undergarment: Now two gowns were worn—the smock and the kirtle. Unmarried women often wore only these two gowns. Buttons, tippets (narrow white bands that flowed from the elbow to ankle), and fitchets (slashes in the kirtle) also came in during this time.

Hose: Same as before.

Shoes: Same as before.

Dress: Called a cote-hardie, and also the sideless surcoat was still worn.

Cloaks: Narrow cloaks fastened with silken cords or brooches began to be worn for state functions. Otherwise, cloaks remained the same.

Hair: Hair was still coiled around the ears and head. Cauls and frets now took on a square shape and were sometimes embroidered. Veils became transparent and very finely woven. Around 1350, a ruffled veil became fashionable.

Fabrics: Silk, satin, velvet, taffeta, scarlet, linen, wool, flannel, russet and canvas.

Colors: Purple, gold, silver, scarlet, murrey, watchet, green, gray, reddish brown, red, light blue, tawny, brown and slate. A reddish orange and a bright tan color came in, but both were expensive.

1377 to 1399

Undergarment: The smock was now also called a chemise. Made from fine linen and silk, it remained unchanged.

Hose: Same as before.

Shoes: Same as before.

Dress: Called a cote-hardie. The surcoat was sideless with the skirt made of a separate material than the bodice. By the end of the reign, women adopted the houppelande. High necked, it was either worn unbelted, or with a high belt that fastened just beneath the breasts.

Cloaks: Same as before.

Hair: Coronets were worn for court or state functions. The square cauls gave way to rounded ones. Chaplets also became fashionable. They were thick, padded, round hats that were embroidered, set with jewels and worn with a veil. During this time, the wimple was relegated to the lower classes.

A cap commonly worn by the poorer classes from 1300 until the end of the Middle Ages.

Fabrics: Silk, freize, satin, velvet, taffeta, scarlet, linen, wool, flannel, russet, canvas and serge.

Colors: Black, purple, scarlet, green, white, gray, red, blue and russet.

1399 to 1413

Undergarment: Same as before.

Hose: Same as before.

Shoes: Same as before.

Dress: The cote-hardie gradually gave way to the houppelande. The front was slit at the neck, and toward the end of the period, a white collar was added that spanned to the shoulders. During this time, the gold and silver S-necklace was worn around the collar of the houppelande.

Belt: Worn just under the breasts.

Cloaks: For state functions they were wide and circular, fastened with silken cords or brooches. It became fashionable to embroider the coats of arms on the back.